Sparking
Innovation

The Lessons Learned Series

Wondering how the most accomplished leaders from around the globe have tackled their toughest challenges? Now you can find out—with Lessons Learned. Concise and engaging, each volume in this new series offers twelve to fourteen insightful essays by top leaders in business, the public sector, and academia on the most pressing issues they've faced.

A crucial resource for today's busy executive, Lessons Learned gives you instant access to the wisdom and expertise of the world's most talented leaders.

Other books in the series:

Leading by Example
Managing Change
Managing Your Career
Managing Conflict
Starting a Business
Hiring and Firing
Making the Sale
Executing for Results

⊰ LESSONS LEARNED ⊱

Sparking Innovation

LES*50*NS

Boston, Massachusetts

Library of Congress Cataloging-in-Publication Data

Sparking innovation.
    p. cm. — (Lessons learned)
  ISBN 978-1-4221-2642-4
  1. New products. 2. Technological innovations—
Management.
  HF5415.153.S657 2008
  658.5'14—dc22

                          2008026042

In partnership with Fifty Lessons, a leading provider of digital media content, Harvard Business School Press is pleased to announce the launch of Lessons Learned, a new book series that showcases the trusted voices of the world's most experienced leaders. Through the power of personal storytelling, each book in this series presents the accumulated wisdom of some of the world's best-known experts and offers insights into how these individuals think, approach new challenges, and use hard-won lessons from experience to shape their leadership philosophies. Organized thematically according to the topics at the top of managers' agendas—leadership, change management, entrepreneurship, innovation, and strategy, to name a few—each book draws from Fifty Lessons' extensive video library of interviews with CEOs and other thought

A Note from the Publisher

leaders. Here, the world's leading senior executives, academics, and business thinkers speak directly and candidly about their triumphs and defeats. Taken together, these powerful stories offer the advice you'll need to take on tomorrow's challenges.

We invite you to join the conversation now. You'll find both new ways of looking at the world, and the tried-and-true advice you need to illuminate the path forward.

⊰ CONTENTS ⊱

Contents

Sparking
Innovation

Hunting for Innovation

Robert Malcolm

President, Global Marketing,
Sales and Innovation, Diageo

SOME OF THE MOST interesting discoveries during my thirty years in this consumer goods business are the nifty places where you can find and source your innovations. The one that particularly comes to mind for me is Sunny Delight, which was a brand that we successfully introduced at

Sparking Innovation

Procter & Gamble in Europe in the late
1990s.

In that particular case, the product sat
right between two categories, almost creating a new category. Juice was on the one
side, soft drinks were on the other side, and
Sunny Delight was a product that resolved
the differences between kids who wanted
soft drinks that weren't good for them and
moms who wanted healthy juice that kids
didn't want to [drink]. Sunny Delight
found a nice hole right in the middle, and
we used the phrase, "Good stuff kids go
for." We found a tremendous source of volume from both of the two categories, but in
a place that didn't step on any other category
that had existed.

The result is, frankly, the most successful
innovation I've been associated with in
more than thirty years. We beat our objec-
tives by more than 200 percent. It was the
most successful beverage launch in the history of Great Britain. The year that it was
launched, which was 1997, it was the most

successful new product launch into all of the grocery trade throughout Europe.

My learning on innovation is that the secret is uncovering an unmet consumer need, either an unmet physical need or perhaps an unmet emotional need, and then filling it in an innovative and creative way. Oftentimes, the most innovative solutions to things come from brilliant solutions to the obvious problems. They're lurking just around the corner.

One of the most innovative territories to look at is the territory in between two categories, where one category is offering one benefit and one category is offering another benefit. By understanding what trade-offs consumers are making between those categories, you often find opportunities for products, and create new categories on the seam of those two. That's a disciplined, logical approach of where you might want to hunt. Solutions for those might be very creative and unique, but the places to hunt usually are not just pie in the sky. [They're not] just creative brainstorms where you wake up in the middle of the night, and all of a sudden, you have a brainstorm for something brand new.

TAKEAWAYS

- The secret to finding innovation lies in uncovering an unmet consumer need and then filling that need in a new and creative way.

- Often, the most innovative solutions come from brilliant solutions to the obvious problems.

- By finding out what trade-offs consumers are making between two categories, it's possible to innovate entirely new categories.

Moving into New Markets

Will Whitehorn

President, Virgin Galactic

LOOKING AT NEW MARKETS in a different way is one of the real lessons of doing business. People tend to think in very sheltered and shuttered ways about what they do.

If you invent the Mars Bar and it's the 1930s, it takes you until the 1980s to think of using the Mars Bar as an ice-cream bar, for example. Now, that may be very rational because Mars becomes so associated with one thing that the Mars family, which invented the name, can't really do much with it. You can't create Mars dog food, for example, because chocolate is bad for dogs. You can't extend that brand much, but you can take it into some new markets. Almost any product name or brand can be taken to new markets.

The unique and interesting thing about the Virgin brand was that very early on in Virgin's history we learned how to look at new markets in a very different way. Richard Branson came up with the brand name in the late 1960s, with the idea of Virgin being a name that could be transferred to other areas, and he had this idea in his mind. I remember finding an interview that he'd done in 1968 for *Vogue* magazine, a piece titled "People of Tomorrow," where at the age of eighteen he talked about how we had called this company Virgin because we're not experienced in business, but we think there are lots of different things we could do for young people in different areas.

Sparking Innovation

That idea, by an eighteen-year-old, is one of the marketing foundations of Virgin—the concept of looking at new markets and looking at them differently. The brand has based its reputation in this area on one big market move that it made to look at a niche market where it felt people were being very badly served, which was the airline industry. Sir Freddie Laker had run an airline in the 1970s that had introduced low-cost, long-haul travel for the first time to the British public. It was about low-cost travel for all and it was cheaper to fly to New York on Laker in 1981 than it was to fly on BA [British Airways] to Paris.

In 1982 that company was bankrupted by a combination of airlines coming together, operating a cartel, and undercutting [Laker] on price. Because the quality of [Laker's] service wasn't very good, Sir Freddie's airline went down. Richard Branson bought that license from the government in late 1983 to launch another airline, and he was always very mindful of what Freddie Laker had experienced.

Sparking Innovation

Branson realized that we had to look at the market to see how the consumer was being badly served and could be better served in the future. He based his idea for that new airline, called Virgin Atlantic, on these simple precepts that Freddie Laker had come out with, that if you're going to enter a new market, you must have a strong brand name, because the public has to recognize the brand. [The public needs to] recognize you as an individual because this is a government-dominated area of business where the government can make rules and changes, and you have to lobby on your behalf and on the consumers' behalf.

He also said that you need to have lots of different price points. You must not just try to be a low-cost airline like Laker, because the business market is very important on long-haul routes. Also, people on long-haul routes tend to fly much more seasonally, so you need to have the different types of marketplace.

You must have a business class, which [Laker] didn't have on his airline, and you

Sparking Innovation

have to be prepared to face a price war from a cartel of airlines and have a better quality of service. If you're going to enter a new market, you have to have a good quality of service. And if you can find a way to do these things, then the sky is the limit.

It doesn't matter if your brand's come out of the music business and is going into the airline business. As long as you have the approach to the marketplace right, the brand can transfer into anything. As long as we were giving the consumer those perceptions of value, quality, and innovation, we could then transfer the brand from place to place. You have to think about what you're doing for the consumer. You have to think about the market niche you're moving across to.

For instance, if we take the idea of Virgin Mobile—it was an idea that came to Richard Branson himself. He was one of the progenitors of this idea in the late 1990s because his kids had prepaid mobiles and they were very expensive to use. His contract mobile, which I think was from Cellnet, as it was called then, was cheaper for him to use. He thought this was very strange because the kids were making quite a lot of calls and there didn't seem to be any mechanism like a normal product, in that the more you used it, the cheaper it got.

We could see at the time of the late 1990s that the market was quite saturated in areas. The business user of the phone, for example, had a complex series of contracts, but this prepaid market was completely undeveloped. Young people who couldn't get credit ratings and didn't have rich parents to get them phones on their contracts were really suffering quite badly. So we decided to find a partner and do a deal whereby we could launch a mobile phone company based upon the simple precept: the more you used the phone every day, the cheaper it got.

Everything was priced incredibly cheaply and simply; and by word of mouth, the concept took off. In four years we got four million customers, and it's just because it's simple, cheap, and easy. It fulfils these ideas of a brand of quality, value for money, and a bit of innovation in the product, and it is simple to use and understandable. If you can keep to those precepts, you can actually move a brand from market to market.

TAKEAWAYS

- People too often think in sheltered ways about what they do. But almost any product name or brand can be taken to new markets.

- To move a brand to a new market, start with a strong brand and provide a level of service that the competition can't match.

- In addition, keep the product or service simple and understandable, and provide strong value for the money.

Innovate by Anticipating Customer Needs

Ivan Seidenberg

CEO, Verizon

Sparking Innovation

IF YOU LOOK AT the last eight, nine, or
ten years, our industry—our company—sits
right in the middle of the juxtaposition between the customer and those who build and
deploy technology. What we have really had
to figure out is how to get closer to the customer. And the closer we get to the customer, the easier it is for us to participate in
the whole idea of innovation, which leads to
growth of the business.

Let's take a couple of examples of what we
do well and what we have learned over the
years. If we look at our business, we've been
in business for a hundred years. We're pri-
marily a business where you pick up the
phone and you make a phone call; you make
a plain old voice call. We've now moved into
an era of data being the dominant service
that we give to customers as well as wireless.

The whole idea of being able to deliver
customer-friendly, value-creating products
and services to customers is something that
we've really had to work very hard on. If
you go back fifteen, twenty years when we

introduced data, we had a hard time figuring out how to get the modems, DSL, and ISDN right. And as I talk, you can see what we have are all technical engineering terms to describe a shift from the voice business to the data business.

We could have innovated faster and better had we been more focused on giving customers what they want. Where we did this much better is in wireless. Wireless is also a voice business, giving people the ability to make phone calls, but the idea of very robust handsets, great coverage, and good-quality service enabled us to create exciting products and services for customers and have made a big difference in the way they saw the company.

Innovation is all about growth. It's all about differentiation. And it really is all about anticipating what the customer's looking for as opposed to what's easy to do when you produce these kinds of new ideas from inside a business. You need to make sure that innovation is driven from the outside in.

Sparking Innovation

How you anticipate needs to drive good services is always a difficult issue, but you have to be a student. You have to be a student of your customers and of the technology, and you have to always put yourself in a position of learning. You need multiple sources within your own company to bring ideas to the middle.

As an executive, what you're always worrying about is making sure you get that right balance. What I notice in our business today is that we get a tremendous amount of input from people who build technology—box manufacturers, consumer electronics, suppliers—and they're always bringing to us what they think are the next great things; but generally it's the next great technical thing. What you find is, if you have your people sitting very close to the customers, you can quickly determine whether or not a given idea has some merit with the marketplace.

The issue for us is to have checks and balances. It's to have a strong marketing and sales organization that speaks to the needs of

the customers in ways that aren't just a re-
flection of what is possible, as it is explained
to us by manufacturers and suppliers.

TAKEAWAYS

- To innovate successfully, you have to get closer to the customer; and the closer you get to the customer, the easier it becomes to participate in the idea of innovation.

- Innovation is about growth, differentiation, and the ability to anticipate what the customer is looking for as opposed to what is easy to do.

- Drive innovation from the outside, where multiple sources contribute ideas about customer needs and how to make those ideas possible.

Moving Beyond Linear Market Research

Neville Isdell

Chairman and CEO,
The Coca-Cola Company

YOU ARE TALKING TO a Coke person. If you want an example of sales and marketing and a great story, you would obviously go to the launch of New Coke. But I'm not going to go there, because that story is well told. Let me give you a more contemporary one, which I was involved in when I came back, and it actually involved Coca-Cola.

We had clearly identified that there was a demand in the diet arena for sweetening a product with Splenda—with sucralose. When I came back, they were developing a product to launch. There was a race to market because our competitors were going in, and there was one competitor already there. We looked at that and said, "Yes, but what's the other piece of the package?"

Well, we have this wonderful new brand name. It's called Coke Zero. We tested out the Zero moniker with Sprite, so marry those together, and we have a winning proposition. But if you'd looked at it a little behind the scenes, you'd see that Splenda actually had quite a severe aftertaste, and that it was going to be a niche [market]. If you looked at the research on Coke Zero, everyone thought that this identified very clearly, particularly with adult males, as a beverage that they would like to drink, could identify with, and, of course, was zero calories.

Sparking Innovation

I said, "Tell me. Here we have a niche. And here we have a very strong brand. Why are we marrying the two?" So we challenged the flavor people to come out with the very best-tasting diet soft drink that we could have, with all of the new research that we had, all of the new IP that we had in terms of being able to dampen the aftertaste of sweeteners, etc. And we came up with a new formula for Coke Zero. That's starting to roll around the world now and has been our greatest success in twenty years, in terms of a launch.

It was just digging down into the detail of what the research showed and actually pushing back on an accommodation. That's what marketers sometimes do in order to come to a result that they were looking for, which is how to best sell a sucralose-sweetened cola. A good question is, what was the trigger for doing that?

The trigger was walking around a major retailer with the buyers, actually looking at other categories that were sweetened with Splenda, and talking to these buyers about how the consumer was reacting to Splenda in these other categories. That was where the learning came from. By understanding that it was a niche in the other categories, it was very clear it would only be a niche for us. It couldn't be anything more than that.

What are the two lessons there? One is collaboration with the customers, because you can get data from them about other categories that you don't have in your normal market research. Your normal market research is pretty well within your own frame of reference and basically linear. You get that broadened frame by talking to the customer.

The other lesson is looking around at other categories. I do it all the time. I wander around a store, and I look at what other people are doing. Where are consumers going in other categories? What are the trends? Get that granular feel.

A lot of it is about intuition, but a lot of it is just about common sense.

Sparking Innovation

TAKEAWAYS

- ⚔ After identifying a demand for a product that satisfies a niche market, develop the best product you can.

- ⚔ Collaborate directly with customers and suppliers to get a broadened frame of reference.

- ⚔ Get into stores and research other market categories to observe consumer trends.

———◆———

The Best Innovations Are New Solutions to Existing Behaviors

———◆———

Andrew Robertson

President and CEO,
BBDO Worldwide

Sparking Innovation

MY BIG A-HA MOMENT, in terms of
our own business, came just over four years
ago when I walked into our study at home,
where my twelve-year-old daughter was
doing her homework.

She was sitting there with the television
on, the laptop on her lap, and her cell
phone [against] her ear. She had a friend
with her, but that's not really important.
She was on the phone to some friends, she
was watching shows, she was flicking between
the shows, and on her computer she had all
of her music. She had instant access through
instant messaging to friends that she was
talking to, one of whom happened to be the
same one who was talking to her on the cell
phone, some of whom happened to be
watching the same shows that she was watching. She had instant access to all of the wonderful things that are available on the
Internet, literally at the click of a button,
millions and millions of sites that she could
go to. And she had games on her computer.

It suddenly dawned on me that this was
the picture of the future. For all the effort

people put into predicting what will happen, maybe we're better off focusing and looking very hard at what is happening. In particular, if you're trying to see what might happen in the future, look at what kids are doing today, because the whole challenge and opportunity of our business was captured in that single image that I had of my daughter doing her homework.

What she was doing is what people have always wanted to do, which is whatever she found interesting. She was flicking between the different sources of information and entertainment, different stimuli that were available to her literally at the touch of a button. As soon as one was no longer interesting, bang, she was onto the next. And she has millions of them to choose from.

If you want to see the future, look at what kids are doing now. If you want to innovate, don't try and think of something new that could be done. Look at what's already happening, and find a way to make it faster, easier, and cheaper.

Sparking Innovation

I found it fascinating because [my daughter is now] sixteen, and she was talking to me about her younger brother, who's fourteen—two years' difference—as another generation because of the way they're using their computers. He and all of his classmates have laptops that have little cameras built into them, and the ease with which you can now video chat is way better than it was two years ago.

They don't instant message now; they video chat. He sits with five of his buddies—a couple of girls, a few guys. They sit and talk now on the screen. Two nights ago he sat watching the first game of the NFL season with his laptop; he had five of his friends on a video chat, and they were all watching the game, but they were talking about it as if they were all there. They were all watching the same game, thirty to forty miles apart from each other, using this new technology.

The point is, six kids watching a football game because they like it better when they watch it with a bunch of people isn't new. But as a piece of innovation, making it easier, faster, and cheaper—it's a whole lot cheaper for them to do this than it is even to move them around and get them to the same place—becomes fantastic innovation. The behavior that created the opportunity for that innovation isn't new.

The best innovation comes from finding new solutions to existing behaviors not from predicting what behaviors will be in the future.

TAKEAWAYS

⊰ Instead of putting your efforts into predicting what the future will bring, focus on what is happening now.

Sparking Innovation

⊰⊱ Take an existing product or service and make it faster, easier, and cheaper. Don't try to invent something new.

⊰⊱ The best innovation comes from finding new solutions to existing be-haviors, not from predicting future behaviors.

Turning Your Customers into Your R&D Force

John Abele

Founder, Boston Scientific

I HAD JUST GRADUATED from college, and I worked for a tiny medical device company where we made scientific instruments. Every year we would go to a trade show called the Federation of American Societies for Experimental Biology. It was the largest sin-

gle scientific meeting in the world at the
time. There was a little company there,
called Technicon, with sales at about $1 mil-
lion. They made pathology equipment, and
I got to know them and Jack Whitehead, the
guy who ran it.

That company was fortunate enough to
meet a physician-scientist who had invented
a product called an automated chemical an-
alyzer. It was dramatically different from
anything else on the market at that time, because it could analyze not just one sample at
a time, but a whole host of samples.

This fellow was going to use it for the
medical field and the societies he worked
with; there was one called the College of
American Pathology and another called the
American Society of Clinical Chemistry.
They were important because they would
make these tests official. Since this was a
proprietary device, if it was made official
then basically the societies would guarantee
a success. Instead, as it turns out, these people couldn't make up their minds which test
they wanted to put onto this machine. He

talked with them for a long time, and they just weren't getting anywhere.

Because it was proprietary, [this physician-scientist] required anybody who was going to buy his machine to come and spend a week at his factory in New York, learning how to use it. That idea of requiring a customer to come and learn was radical at the time, but in fact what happened was that he made friends with all of them. At that time of the early 1960s, he created a cult of users. I say a "cult" of users because they knew each other. They were all pioneers, and they started communicating with each other long before the Internet.

That ability to get to know the customers, to stimulate them not only to learn how to use the machine but also to develop new tests on their own, impressed me a great deal. He wasn't simply building and selling a product—he wasn't even creating a market—he was creating a field.

I was impressed because he had made his customers his R&D force. And it wasn't just a few people; it was a large group. I was struck by the lesson to develop a really deep relationship with your customers. They're not just customers; they're really partners in understanding the field that you're developing together.

Over time, they will become your R&D force, and maybe they'll advance the field. Other companies will come out of it, and that's okay. At the end of the day, the field will be much larger, and you will do much better as a result. You'll have people who are not only proud of making a product but also who are proud of contributing to a field.

TAKEAWAYS

⊰ When innovating in a new field, get to know your customers and develop a relationship with them.

Sparking Innovation

⚜ Doing so creates a partnership,
whereby customers can actually become your R&D force.

⚜ By working together, you can advance
an entire field, creating an even larger
market for your product.

Successfully Implementing New Technology

Clayton Christensen

*Robert and Jane Cizik Professor
of Business Administration,
Harvard Business School*

WHEN YOU HAVE A NEW technology,
almost always the successful implementation
of the new technology comes when you
compete against nonconsumption—use the

technology in an application where previously the customer's only alternative was nothing at all. That way, the new technology can delight the customer, and all it has to do is be better than nothing.

If you try to implement a new technology into an established system, the only way it can be used there is if it's better than the old way of doing things in those applications. Typically, there is a very onerous technical hurdle to overcome there, whereas here all you have to do is make something better than nothing.

You see this happening in the past and today—for example, when the transistor disrupted the vacuum tube. RCA, the leading consumer electronics company at the time, and the vacuum-tube product manufacturers all took licenses to the transistor from RCA. But it couldn't be used in the market that existed for consumer electronics in the '50s and '60s. These were huge floor-standing televisions and tabletop radios.

So they took their licenses to the transistor into their own labs. In today's dollars, they spent well over a billion dollars trying to make the transistor good enough that it could handle the power required to make big, floor-standing TVs and radios.

While they were working on that problem, Sony came into the market with a very different orientation and made a very cheap, simple pocket radio that sold for $2.00. Teenagers were delighted to have this crummy, simple pocket radio because it was infinitely better than no radio at all, which was the alternative they'd been living with. I was raised in Salt Lake City, and I remember when I had my first Sony radio. I actually had to stand facing west, which was where the radio tower was, in order to catch the signal. It was really a crummy product.

Sony went next to little portable televisions that were so cheap and simple that people whose wallets weren't big enough to buy a big floor-standing RCA TV or whose apartments weren't large enough to have a big floor-standing TV now could have this little thing. And because it was infinitely better than nothing, customers were delighted.

Sparking Innovation

Ultimately then, solid-state electronics, commercialized by Sony and others, got to the point that now they could start to make big TVs and radios with it. And then all the customers got sucked out of the vacuum-tube world into the new. And every vacuum-tube company got vaporized.

This happens over and over again in our studies of innovation. The leaders typically try to cram the disruptive technology into head-on competition with the old technology in the market that they serve. If you want to commercialize it successfully and create new growth, you have to come out and use the technology to make inexpensive simple products that are infinitely better than nothing.

TAKEAWAYS

⚔ To succeed in new technologies, the best competition is nonconsumption. That is, use the technology in a product where the customer's alternative is nothing.

⚔ Even if the new product is "crummy," it will be infinitely better than nothing and will delight customers.

⚔ Starting with an inexpensive, simple product will bring more success than going head-to-head against the competition to find different uses for old technologies.

Don't Let Success Stifle Fresh Thinking

Robert Herbold

Former Chief Operating Officer,
Microsoft Corporation

ONE OF THE KEY LESSONS I learned at Procter & Gamble in the middle of my career was just how important it is to be able to constantly look for new ways to do the work you're charged to do and add value to the organization.

Procter & Gamble had an incredible experience with Sam Walton on this issue. Back in 1987 Sam Walton came to the CEO of Procter & Gamble and said, "You are really good at total quality." Total quality was the precursor to Six Sigma, so it's all about process improvement. Sam asked, "Could you assemble a team of your boys to come down to Bentonville, Arkansas, and teach us some of these fancy techniques so that we can be sure to keep our company up to date?"

The CEO of Procter & Gamble puffed out his chest and said, "Of course." He was very proud of what they'd been doing in total quality. So he assembled the team, and I happened to be included. I was the CIO at that point, so I was in charge of the Information Technology area. We go down to Bentonville with the total quality trainer, and he comes in with this huge stack of transparencies and starts droning through them one at a time.

Sparking Innovation

After about an hour, Sam gets up and says, "I think I'm beginning to understand this total quality stuff, and I have a problem that we need to be working on now." He didn't ask any more questions; he just went to the easel and took a felt-tipped pen and started drawing boxes like crazy. He then explains to the group that his task is very simple. It's taking too long to reorder product from Procter & Gamble. It's requiring too many people on his part. And it creates inventories that are too large. What he wants to do is simply hook the Procter & Gamble computers to the Wal-Mart computers.

He then points out that Procter & Gamble has seven operating divisions, so they have seven sales organizations. Each of them has different practices, and each of them comes to Bentonville, sits in Sam's lobby, and waits for a long time to see Sam's buyer. And Sam has to have buyers to interface with all of them. They sit there and make a bunch of arithmetic mistakes that later need to be repaired. Sam gets inventories that are too large because salespeople are too good at

selling the buyer too much merchandise.
And he just wants to get rid of this problem.
He thinks by letting the machines do it, that
we'd be a lot better off.

We—the Procter crew—were absolutely
speechless, but we realized that there was no
way we were going to get the meeting back,
so we began to work with Sam on his problem. We got the thing up and running, went
to work on disposable diapers, and at the
end of eleven weeks, we had a meeting with
Sam back in Bentonville. Sam got this big
grin on his face and asked, "How did you
boys do?" And we said, "It was shocking. We
moved from 20 turns a year up to 120 turns
a year on disposable diapers." Now 120
turns in a one-year period means, on aver-
age, Sam had the product about three days.

The thing was a raging success. We expanded it to the other products within Wal-
Mart. We assembled a twelve-person sales
team that handled all of the Wal-Mart business, and Wal-Mart was 10 percent of Procter & Gamble's volume at that point. We
expanded this system to other accounts—we

being Procter & Gamble—and eventually, after two or three years, we were able to decrease the size of the sales organization by about 45 percent.

You step back and ask, "What went on here?" Well, Sam had to teach us a lesson in creativity. Why couldn't Procter & Gamble think of that? The reason is, they were fairly successful. They were doing fine. They were gaining [revenues] and profit of about 7 percent each annually, which was good, steady performance. It's what shareholders wanted.

So what's the crisis? People just operated in their silos, coming at Sam from all different angles—complicating his life—and the Procter & Gamble salespeople never thought about what that looked like from a customer standpoint.

The lesson is, when you're doing well, your ability to think creative thoughts is really degraded. You constantly need to keep in front of you the fact that you're probably being blindsided. You're probably being naive that there aren't great ways to run that railroad better than you're running it today.

One of the things you note with organizations that have had some degree of success is that people get very proud, and they get protective of their legacy practices because that's what brought them to their level of success. There are two ways to deal with that issue. Number one is to somehow get the individual to understand that the issue at hand is constant improvement. The other way to deal with it is to rotate people and put fresh talent in the job, because if you get smart folks who have a good head on their shoulders and put them in just about any job, it takes them about two months to figure out the lay of the land. And by the fourth month, they're coming up with all kinds of fresh, new thinking as to ways to do it better.

TAKEAWAYS

⚔ Constantly looking for new ways to do your work and add value to the organization is key to successful innovation.

⚔ When a company is successful, however, its creativity is degraded, and its people become protective of legacy practices because it's what made them successful.

⚔ To combat these issues, focus on putting fresh talent into the company and always strive for ways to do things better.

Avoid Rigid Thinking

Jimmy Wales

Founder, Wikipedia,
Wikimedia Foundation

THE HISTORY OF WIKIPEDIA can tell
something about rule breaking having great
impact. Before Wikipedia I had a project
called Nupedia. Nupedia had the same broad
vision, the same idea that excited people,
which was to create a free encyclopedia for
every single person on the planet, in their

own languages. That broad, unifying idea got a lot of people excited, and they came in to start working on this.

The model we designed at that time was very top-down. There was a seven-stage review process in which people had to fax in their degrees so that they could prove their credentials. The process was very old-fashioned, but it was also old-fashioned for a reason. It wasn't old-fashioned just because we wanted to be old-fashioned; it was old-fashioned because we thought that's how you would build an encyclopedia. This was a complete failure. We put a ton of money into it and two years of really hard work, and we had very little to show for it.

Then we discovered the wiki editing idea, which had been around for several years at that time. Wikis were an online phenomenon. [But they were] low-key. A few programmers were using wikis; it was a subculture.

Harnessing that idea and saying, "Okay, let's take this completely radically open thing and start building an encyclopedia with that," was really contrary to everything that we previously thought would work. And it grew—we didn't just randomly decide it—out of my frustration in talking with the volunteers who were trying to build the encyclopedia. What's wrong? Why is it taking so long? So I said, "Let's just blow all that away and have a totally open-ended model instead of a priori figuring out what we think the right path is. Then, as we see problems arise, we'll think about how to solve them."

As it turned out, partly because our community grew out of the dot-com crash, there was no funding. Anytime a problem arose where we naturally thought we needed to have staff members to do X or Y, there were no staff members. We had to evolve ways for the community to do it. That's what really led us, as an ever-growing and large group, to this model of radically open-ended, radical content generation by the general public.

One of the main lessons that I draw out of the story of the transition from Nupedia to Wikipedia is to avoid excessive a priori thinking. We had a lot of ideas about what this project would look like, how we would create an encyclopedia, and tried to a priori design the whole thing to match that preset idea. It turns out we were wrong about several things and right about a few things. The excessive a priori thinking led us to believe we had to proceed in a certain route, which we didn't.

The lesson that I learned from that is— whenever possible—if you don't have to make a decision today, then don't. Wait. Leave things open-ended and try to pursue a path so that you can make that decision at a future juncture when you need to. This has a broad applicability in many contexts. If you a priori imagine everything and then you pursue it in a very rigid way, you can get off track before you can realize it and never get back.

TAKEAWAYS

- Top-down models and old-fashioned processes can stifle innovation. In such cases, breaking the rules can have great impact.

- Develop an open-ended model instead of a priori figuring out what you think the right path is. Solve problems as you encounter them.

- If you don't have to make a decision today, then don't. Make those decisions in the future, when you need to.

Managing Innovation Internally

Matt Ferguson

CEO, CareerBuilder.com

THE CHALLENGE WHEN YOU'RE looking at innovation is to decide when to partner and rely on outside companies or outside consultants and when to rely on internal people to do the innovation. That's a tough decision to make, but that's usually the first decision you should make.

I can think of a particular example when we were thinking about a recommendation or a matching engine within our business. Think about our business; it's mass data, right? We have a lot of job seekers and a lot of jobs, and you have to match those up effectively. There were a lot of outside vendors that were coming to us all the time talking about how they could apply technology across our systems that would help us do that more effectively. That's a very compelling sales pitch, but at the end of the day, we believed it was too important—too integral to our business—to outsource that.

We dedicated a team of individuals within CareerBuilder.com, and we asked them to try and solve that very difficult problem. We said that we were going to give them three months with very little direction, just very high-level. We wanted [the team] to provide us with a matching technology that allowed more qualified applicants to apply for the jobs [posted by] our customers. We wanted this team to come back in three months and show us that they'd made progress. And they did.

We gave them very broad direction, and we gave them three months; and we left them alone. We didn't give them six months; we didn't give them a year. We didn't ask them to reinvent the world. But during that three-month period, we wanted to show an iterative improvement with the use of matching technology. They came back in three months and they said, "Here's what we've learned. Here's where we can show improvement and here's where we can't." We said, "Let's agree to these three things; come back in another three months."

Within a year we were getting 40 percent of our applicants on our site; I would say our applicants were up about 45 or 46 percent. It was all internally done, all within this group, and all giving them three-month cycles using iterative improvements to what our systems could do at that time. We continue to see success today, and we think we will in the next twelve months from that same process.

When you're looking at innovation within a company, the first thing that we always look at is whether we going to bring in some people from the outside to help in this innovation process. You identify something—a particular area of the business you want to try innovation on—and then you decide whether you need outside help or whether you can do this internally.

If you decide to do it internally, the next step is to give very broad directives, not specific business requirements that are three pages long or twenty pages long, but very broad business directives. Then ask [your people], in a very short cycle but at least three months, to come back to the business with an improvement within that area. Again, it may be different for you and your particular business in your particular area of innovation. Still, you have to give a short amount of time for the team to show

progress but not so long that they can continue to flounder.

The important thing that you want to do,
especially in the technology business, is get
it out to the market to get feedback. You
don't want to innovate too long away from
the market and the response of the market.
The great thing about Internet business is,
in our case, you put it out there and very
quickly you get feedback; does this work or
does this not work?

Allow a time for innovation, apart from
the marketplace, reaction from the marketplace, and then [allow time for] more innovation around it. Then decide whether you
need further help from outside vendors in
this process or whether you can continue to
do it internally.

TAKEAWAYS

- ⚜ The first decision to be made when undertaking innovation is to determine whether to innovate internally or partner with others. Realize, however, that innovation may be too important to outsource.

- ⚜ To innovate internally, create a focused team that has a broad direction and give them three months to show iterative improvement.

- ⚜ At that point, reevaluate where the project stands, get market feedback, and allow time for additional innovation. Then decide whether to continue internally.

Implementing Innovation in a Risk-Averse Culture

Jim Garrity

*Former Chief Marketing Officer,
Wachovia*

Sparking Innovation

AT WACHOVIA, in early 2005, we
reached a profound conclusion that we
could no longer grow by simply acquiring
customers by acquiring the institutions
that had relationships with them. We were
going to have to grow organically, meaning
we would have to grow by acquiring one customer at a time. We also came to the realiza-
tion that innovation was going to be the way
we were going to have to do that.

We felt we were not innovative at the time,
and felt what we needed to do was make a
concerted effort to study how best practices
companies do it—in financial services; and
more importantly, outside of financial services—how they drive innovation in their
companies.

We did two things, starting in 2005. We
formed a cross-functional core team to
drive this effort, and then came up with the
idea, in early 2006, to leverage a resource
that was going to be available to us.

Every year, there are one or more executive leadership program classes taught at

Sparking Innovation

Wachovia. It's for up-and-coming midlevel executives. Every year, they're given an action learning assignment, something that will actually have a benefit to the corporation when we harness the power that comes from these thirty employees, who have enormous experience across the enterprise and tremendous brainpower.

In August of 2006, we launched the class and the action learning assignment. This is a class that meets once a week for five straight months. We took the thirty members of this class in partnership with the core team and gave them an assignment: study how innovation is done at the most innovative companies in this country and then make a recommendation for a model that would work at Wachovia, to culminate—they found this out on August 16—in a presentation to the CEO and his operating committee on January 31, 2007, the last day of the ELP program.

One of the things that we tried to do to really symbolize innovation was use nontraditional methods of communication with the class. We basically outlawed PowerPoint as a vehicle to be used, to get them to think differently about how they communicate. The teams within the ELP class created their own audio and video podcasts.

We used collaboration tools, both from the universities we worked with and with IBM, to get them all understanding how innovative companies collaborate. We did exhaustive best practices, benchmarking against some of the leaders that typically get high praise, well-deserved praise—companies like Procter & Gamble, General Electric, and Dell—and got tremendous learnings from them. We found some consistencies across how they drove innovation in their companies—the role that culture played—tremendous learnings that all factored their way into the ultimate recommendation that was made to the operating committee.

Now, their recommendation to the operating committee, also symbolically, was very

nontraditional. [Besides outlawing] Power-
Point, we also brought in Second City.
Second City is the comedy troupe company
out of Chicago that actually created the
idea for *Saturday Night Live*; they are the
founders and fathers of *Saturday Night
Live*. And over a period of weeks, they
coached the presentation team, such that
the final presentation actually was a series
of sketches that were acted out by the team.
The content of the presentation, or the
sketches, and then the impact of the tech-
nique, resulted in, literally, a standing
ovation from the CEO and the operating
committee, and an instant endorsement of
the recommendation.

Since [the class's] recommendation was
made in January 2007, it's actually been
implemented. In April of the same year,
a new infrastructure was put in place, an
innovation center was announced, and
an innovation center leader position was
announced. They're in the process of
building that infrastructure right today.

Sparking Innovation

We had a lot of learnings along the way. It started with the acknowledgement of the fact, in 2005, that we really were not innovative. That took a cold stare into the mirror to say, "You know what? We're not innovative." We also didn't have a process and infrastructure. We had thousands of employees who had extremely creative and wonderful ideas, and they just didn't know where to take them. There was no one central place you could go. If you had a big idea that would work across many business units in the company, you couldn't find any one business unit that would get excited about it, because its breadth was the beauty of it all, but each business unit was focused on their bottom-line result.

Those were important needs that we felt we had to address, and we did need to move along the learning curve quite quickly. The fact that we acknowledged we were not innovative was a big plus for us. We also acknowledged that we had some elements of our culture that were inhibiting innovation.

Sparking Innovation

One was because of the business we're in;
we're highly risk-averse in financial services.

Innovative companies take risks. Innovative companies celebrate risks; they celebrate the learnings that come from risks, not the fact that someone failed. Innovative companies that are very good at this also have a method of failing fast, learning quickly from the failing, and then moving on without overcommitting resources to something that looks like it's not a promising idea.

TAKEAWAYS

- Innovation is one of the keys to growing organically. In a risk-averse culture, this can be a challenge.

- To overcome this obstacle, you need to symbolize innovation within the company itself. For example, intro-

Sparking Innovation

duce nontraditional methods into communications and recognize those elements that inhibit innovation.

⇥ Learn to take risks. When you succeed, celebrate; when you fail, learn from your mistakes.

Creativity and Routine Work Are Hard to Mix

Robert Sutton

*Professor of Management
Science and Engineering,
Stanford University*

Sparking Innovation

THIS LESSON IS ONE that I came across while I was doing research on a book that I was writing called *Weird Ideas That Work*. I was looking at creative organizations—how you build one and what can get in the way. I had breakfast with Mitch Kapoor, the founder of a company called Lotus. He's this old hippie, like a "frumpled," accidental billionaire; in fact he's sort of the poster child for the accidental billionaire.

He told me this astounding story about how, after he had founded Lotus, essentially with a few hippies, they wrote a spreadsheet program and it started selling quickly. It had been a company of just a few people; then he looked around, and there were three or four thousand people. Mitch was chairman of this giant company. One of the things that I remember in particular that he emphasized was, "I was used to creative hippies and then I was surrounded by marketing guys from Procter & Gamble wearing white shirts and suits. I couldn't understand a word they were saying."

Sparking Innovation

Mitch [has] a multibillion-dollar company; he has a CEO from McKinsey, and he
can't quite figure out what's going on. First,
he was amazed that they were selling all this
software; and second, he was disgusted by
the lack of creativity of these people.

With his Head of Organizational Development, Freada Klein, the woman who is
now his wife, Mitch took the résumés for the
first forty people who started the company,
including his own. They changed the names,
put them into the human resource management system and saw which ones would get
hired by the company. Even though they had
job openings for which a good thirty of
those people were qualified, they didn't get
call-backs because they had funny things in
their résumés. They'd spent a year traveling
around the country, lived on an Ashram,
or—like Mitch—they'd taken transcendental
meditation; that's where the name Lotus
came from. The creative people who had
started the company couldn't even get a
call-back.

Sparking Innovation

If you fast-forward through the history of Lotus, they only ever had one successful product after the spreadsheet program—Lotus Notes. The only way that had been possible was through Mitch giving a guy named Ray Ozzie some money to pull him out of the rigid stifling corporate structure that just wanted to sell things and not do anything creative.

This is an astounding story of how a machine that can sell something can completely drive out creativity. The difference between creative work and routine work really does require different sorts of people in different sorts of processes. Those same people who made the company possible would not have been particularly good at selling the stuff in a routine sales pitch; but in the process of bringing aboard so many people who are so great at sales, they wouldn't bring in people like themselves.

One of the best—and most consistent—findings in behavioral sciences is this thing called "homosocial reproduction," a concept from Rosabeth Moss Kanter. This is essentially the idea that we love our favorite person. Who is our favorite person? Ourselves. We mindlessly search for people like ourselves and automatically reject people who are different. That's what happened at Lotus. It started out with the creative types, but once they started bringing in all those people who could sell and do routine work, it drove out the creative types.

The lesson isn't that those people from Procter & Gamble were bad and the old hippies that Mitch loved so much were good. Hippies aren't the only people who are creative; that's the last thing I'd want to say. The lesson is that there are different sorts of logic in different approaches to routine versus innovative work.

TAKEAWAYS

- To build an innovative company, you have to know what can get in the way. Rigid corporate structures can drive out creativity by hiring too many like-minded people.

- This happens because people have a natural tendency to like people who are like themselves and reject people who are different.

- The difference between innovative work and routine work are the types of people who do the work. As the company gets larger, take care to hire with an eye toward diversity.

Workers and Innovators

Phil Smith

Business Development Director,
Cisco Systems, UK & Ireland

THIS LESSON IS ABOUT the makeup
of teams, particularly leadership management teams that are trying to lead a company
or part of a company. You have to have a
particular mix of lots of attributes, but there
are two key attributes.

Sparking Innovation

One of them really is an innovator, and by an innovator I mean someone who is able to make change, someone who dares to make change; a person who comes up with the ideas. Maybe some of those ideas are less than practical, but this person comes up with the ideas, continually challenging things.

The other core skill that I believe you need to have in people in a leadership team is basically a hard worker, or, as we might say in the United Kingdom, a *grafter*—somebody who just puts in the time and drives through on pure effort of their own.

Now, someone who drives and works like that, if they don't have any other capabilities, of course isn't necessarily someone you have in a team. I think there's a basic level of assuming that these people are capable managers who have some proven track record and so on. What you ultimately need to have is either people who are workers or people who are innovators; in fact the ideal combination is to have someone who is both.

Sparking Innovation

In the big successful companies—the
IBMs of the world, ICL in older times, and
Digital in others—there are huge amounts of
innovation within them as they've grown.
But as they got toward the times when they
started to struggle in satisfying some of their
customer demands, maybe they didn't have
such a strong work ethic or strong drive and
graft within the management team; maybe
they developed a bit of complacency.

When I worked in IBM, I had small teams
of people who were tremendously innovative
and who were creating whole new ways of
doing business and challenging the external
marketplace. Looking back about thirteen
years ago, I had people on my team who
were looking at setting up Internet capability for the whole of Europe. There was no
such thing as Internet capability for the
whole of Europe at that time except in the
education space. The problem was that it
was completely innovative, and what we
didn't have in that particular team were all
the people who knew how to put the work in

to actually deliver that. And IBM culturally didn't quite match that at the time, to be fair.

If you have innovators in the leadership team, they tend to encourage innovation within the rest of the organization as well. If the leadership team has neither hard workers nor particular innovators, it's very difficult to build that culture within your organization.

I try, within my team, to encourage innovation. I try to allow people to stretch what they're doing sometimes and test the edges a bit. But it has to be backed up with the practicality of actually being able to deliver. That's something that can be done as part of a team. The point is that, unless it's done at the senior team, you're on light footing throughout the rest of the organization.

TAKEAWAYS

- In leadership management teams, it's important to have both innovators and workers.

- An innovator is someone who is able to make change, someone who dares to make change, a person who comes up with ideas. A worker is someone who puts in the time and drives through on their own effort.

- By putting together a leadership team that is both innovative and able to deliver, you can build a similar, successful culture throughout the entire organization.

The Future

Sir David Varney

Executive Chairman,
HM Revenue and Customs

I JOINED SHELL in 1968, and a few weeks after I'd arrived, one of the senior managers took me into a room and explained what the future would be like. The way he explained it was how he had experienced Shell over the last forty years, which had seen phenomenal growth.

A couple of days later, I realized that all the personnel material with which I'd been presented was about projecting the past into the future. It was a wake-up call; in big corporations, if you're not careful, the past just carries you forward into a place where the past is irrelevant.

The most difficult thing in an organization is to understand how much of the past you should take forward, and what you should invent for the future. The past forty years for the oil industry had been all about growth. More and more energy had been consumed; more of it was oil, which had replaced coal. Some of us could begin to see a world in which energy demand would not be as strong. All of the tactics based on growth were not going to get us to success; that was one thing. The other is that we'd gone from being in twenty countries to being in forty, then in sixty. If you drew the line infinitely, we would have colonized Pluto; clearly there was nobody there and no demand, so at some point we had to change the way the organization thought.

Sparking Innovation

Most of the future is around us today. A lot of the trends have changed, and we haven't caught up. So it's partly being aware of what is happening to the demand for your product or service. It's also about exposing the assumptions that are built into the everyday culture of the company to those who probably know it best, spending time describing where we think we're going and testing whether that's where they think they're going.

I like to understand what the assumptions are in the culture, who the heroes are, what people think the future is going to look like, and how much of that is a repeat of the past. If you're not careful when you talk to people, if you don't set out a new view of the future, they go into the future looking at the past. They retain things that were relevant in the past, which becomes a real barrier to meeting the expectations of customers and stakeholders in the future.

It's talking about what is changing in the here-and-now and why. How much do we understand about what customers want? What's causing them to change their behavior? Once you start to get into that sort of dialogue, it's amazing how many people contribute insights that are important for the company. Otherwise you're driving a big company by looking in the rearview mirror. If you've ever tried driving a fast car around a race circuit looking at the rear view mirror, it isn't long before you crash.

TAKEAWAYS

- ⇥ In big corporations, projecting the past into the future just carries you forward into a place where the past is irrelevant.

- ⇥ To succeed, you need to find the balance between how much of the past

Sparking Innovation

you should take forward and what you should invent for the future.

⚏ Be aware of what is happening to the demand for your product or service and be willing to expose the assumptions that are built into your everyday culture. The future is around you today.

⚔ ABOUT THE ⚔
CONTRIBUTORS

John Abele is the Co-Founder of Boston Scientific Corporation, the worldwide developer, manufacturer, and marketer of medical devices. Mr. Abele has been driving the advancement of less-invasive medical technology for more than twenty-five years.

Boston Scientific's history goes back to the late 1960s, when Mr. Abele acquired an equity interest in Medi-tech Inc., a research and development company focused on developing alternatives to traditional surgery, where he served as President. In 1979 Mr. Abele partnered with Pete Nicholas to buy Medi-tech, and together they formed Boston Scientific Corporation. Since its public offering in 1992, Boston Scientific has undergone an aggressive acquisition strategy, assembling the lines of business that allow it to continue to be a leader in the medical industry. Mr. Abele has been a Director of Boston Scientific since 1979.

Mr. Abele serves as Director of Color Kinetics, Inc., a leader in designing and marketing innovative lighting systems based on light emitting diode (LED) technology. He has held the Chairmanship of FIRST (For Inspiration and Recognition of Science and Technology) Foundation since 2002.

About the Contributors

Clayton Christensen is the Robert and Jane Cizik Professor of Business Administration at the Harvard Business School, with a joint appointment in the Technology & Operations Management and General Management faculty groups. His research and teaching interests center on managing innovation and creating new growth markets. He has been a faculty member since 1992.

A seasoned entrepreneur, Professor Christensen has founded three successful companies. The first, CPS Corporation, is an advanced materials manufacturing company that he founded in 1984 with several MIT professors. The second, Innosight, is a consulting and training company focused on problems of strategy, innovation, and growth that Christensen founded with several of his former students in 2000. Innosight Capital, the third firm, was launched in 2005. From 1979 to 1984, he worked with The Boston Consulting Group (BCG). In 1982 Professor Christensen was named a White House Fellow, and he served as assistant to U.S. Transportation Secretaries Drew Lewis and Elizabeth Dole.

Professor Christensen holds a BA with highest honors in economics from Brigham Young University, and an MPhil in applied econometrics and the economics of less-developed countries from Oxford University, where he studied as a Rhodes Scholar. He received an MBA with high distinction from the Harvard Business School, graduating as a George F. Baker Scholar. He was awarded his DBA from the Harvard Business School in 1992.

About the Contributors

Professor Christensen is the author or coauthor of five books, and his writings have won a number of awards.

Matt Ferguson is the CEO of CareerBuilder.com, the largest online job site in the United States, with more than 25 million unique visitors and more than 1.6 million jobs.

In his role as CEO, which he assumed in 2002, Mr. Ferguson leads the daily operations and growth of the company, overseeing sales, finance, marketing, information technology, product development, integrated media, business development, customer care, and human resources. Under his leadership, CareerBuilder.com has risen to the number-one position in online recruitment with the company outpacing the industry in traffic, job postings, and revenue growth.

Mr. Ferguson first joined the company following CareerBuilder.com's acquisition of Headhunter .net, where he had been serving as Senior Vice President of Business Development. Before that, he developed strategic partnerships for DigitalWork.com. He also started two entrepreneurial ventures and practiced law at Baker & McKenzie.

Mr. Ferguson is an employment expert who regularly appears on national TV and radio to discuss the state of the job market, hiring practices, and workplace issues.

Jim Garrity is the former Chief Marketing Officer and Executive Vice President at Wachovia, one of the top financial services corporations in the United States. He is currently retired.

Mr. Garrity began his career at IBM, where he worked in various sales and marketing positions. When he left IBM in 1992, he was the Director of Advertising, IBM US. Mr. Garrity then joined Compaq, where he was charged with various advertising and marketing roles. While at Compaq, he served as Vice President of Communications.

From 1997 to 2001 he served as Executive Vice President and Chief Marketing Officer at First Union in Charlotte, North Carolina. When First Union merged with Wachovia in 2001, he led the company's rebranding efforts with the new name, Wachovia. Mr. Garrity held this position until his retirement in July 2007.

Mr. Garrity was Director of the Association of National Advertisers, Inc. (ANA) from 1995 to 2007 and was Chairman in 1998. From 1996 to 2007 Mr. Garrity also served as Director of the Ad Council.

Robert Herbold is the former Chief Operating Officer and Executive Vice President of Microsoft Corporation and is the Managing Director of the consulting business Herbold Group, LLC.

Mr. Herbold joined Microsoft in 1994 as Chief Operating Officer and Executive Vice President. For the following six-and-a-half years, he was responsible for finance, manufacturing and distribution, information systems, human resources, corporate marketing, market research, and public relations. During his tenure as COO, Microsoft experienced a four-fold increase in revenue and a seven-fold increase in profits.

From spring 2001 until June 2003 Mr. Herbold worked part time for Microsoft as Executive Vice President, assisting in the government, industry, and customer areas.

Prior to his time at Microsoft, Mr. Herbold spent twenty-six years at Procter & Gamble. During his last five years with P&G, he was Senior Vice President of Advertising and Information Services, responsible for the company's worldwide advertising and brand management operations, all marketing related services, and management information systems worldwide.

Mr. Herbold serves as Director of Agilent Technologies, Indachin Ltd. Hong Kong, and First Mutual Bank. He recently authored the books *The Fiefdom Syndrome* and *Seduced by Success: How the Best Companies Survive the 9 Traps of Winning.*

In 2001 Mr. Herbold was appointed by President George W. Bush to the President's Council of Advisors on Science and Technology. He currently chairs the Council's education subcommittee.

E. Neville Isdell is the current Chairman and Chief Executive Officer of The Coca-Cola Company, a position he has held since June 2004.

About the Contributors

Mr. Isdell joined The Coca-Cola Company in 1966 with the local bottling company in Zambia. In 1972 he became general manager of Coca-Cola Bottling of Johannesburg. Mr. Isdell was named Region Manager for Australia in 1980, and in 1981 he became President of the bottling joint venture between The Coca-Cola Company and San Miguel Corporation in the Philippines, where he oversaw the turnaround and renewal of the Coca-Cola business in that key country.

Mr. Isdell became President of the company's Central European Division in 1985. In 1989 he was elected Senior Vice President of the company and appointed President of the Northeast Europe/Africa Group (renamed the Northeast Europe/Middle East Group in 1992) and led the Company's entry into new markets in India, the Middle East, Eastern Europe, and the former Soviet Union. In 1995 he was named President of the Greater Europe Group.

From July 1998 to September 2000 Mr. Isdell served as Chairman and CEO of Coca-Cola Beverages, Plc. in Great Britain, where he oversaw that company's merger with Hellenic Bottling to form the world's second largest Coca-Cola bottler at the time, Coca-Cola Hellenic Bottling Company (HBC). He retired as Vice Chairman of Coca-Cola HBC in December 2001. From January 2002 to May 2004, Mr. Isdell was an international consultant to The Coca-Cola Company and headed his own investment company in Barbados.

About the Contributors

Mr. Isdell is Chairman of the U.S.-Russia Business Council and Chairman of the board of trustees of the International Business Leaders Forum (IBLF). He is a member of the board of trustees of the United States Council for International Business and the Center for Strategic and International Studies. He is also a member of the Corporate Advisory Board of the Global Business Coalition on HIV/AIDS. In Atlanta, Mr. Isdell serves as Director of Sun Trust Banks, Inc.

Robert Malcolm is President of Global Marketing, Sales, and Innovation for the London-based Diageo, Plc., which produces and distributes a collection of branded premium spirits, beer, and wine. He has held this position since September 2000.

Before joining Diageo, Mr. Malcolm served as Scotch Category Director and then Global Marketing Director with United Distillers & Vintners. He also held various marketing and general management positions with The Procter & Gamble Company from 1975 to 2000.

Since June 2007 Mr. Malcolm has also served as Director of Logitech, Inc., a manufacturer of computer control devices.

Andrew Robertson is President and Chief Executive Officer of BBDO Worldwide (part of Omnicom Group), which provides creative development and management services for some of the world's leading brands.

About the Contributors

Mr. Robertson began his advertising career at Ogilvy & Mather Worldwide (a subsidiary of WPP Group, Plc.) as a Media Planner. He switched to Account Management and was appointed to the board of Ogilvy & Mather in 1986.

In 1989 he joined J. Walter Thompson as a member of the Management Group, and in November 1990 he was appointed Chief Executive of WCRS.

Mr. Robertson moved to BBDO in 1995, joining Abbott Mead Vickers BBDO. There he served as Chief Executive. In 2001 he moved to BBDO North America to serve as President and CEO. In 2002 he became President of BBDO Worldwide, and in 2004 he became CEO of BBDO Worldwide.

He currently serves on the boards of the Advertising Council, Inc. and the American Association of Advertising Agencies.

Ivan Seidenberg is Chairman of the Board and Chief Executive Officer of the premier network company Verizon.

Mr. Seidenberg was instrumental in forming Verizon through a number of mergers and acquisitions. He has led Verizon since its inception, first as co-CEO in 2000, then as sole CEO since 2002, and Chairman since 2004.

Before the creation of Verizon, Mr. Seidenberg was Chairman and CEO of Bell Atlantic and NYNEX. He began his communications career more than forty years ago as a cable splicer's assis-

About the Contributors

tant and has held numerous operations and engineering assignments, including various leadership positions at NYNEX and Bell Atlantic.

In 2007 President George W. Bush named him to the National Security Telecommunications Advisory Committee, which advises the president on communications issues related to national security, emergency preparedness, and the protection of critical infrastructure.

Mr. Seidenberg also serves as director of Honeywell International, Inc.; the Museum of Television and Radio; the New York Hall of Science; Pace University; Verizon Foundation; and Wyeth.

Phil Smith is the Head of Technology & Corporate Marketing, Europe. Mr. Smith's career path includes working for IBM Corp. and Philips Industries in various senior roles, including design and implementation of some of today's largest networks.

Mr. Smith joined Cisco in a consultancy role in 1994 and has been with Cisco for more than nine years. He was formerly the Business Development Director for Cisco UK & Ireland, where he was responsible for market development, technical strategy, and alliances. He also drives Cisco's local investment and acquisition activities.

Mr. Smith is a frequent public speaker on Internet, e-business, and strategy issues, and he is a regular correspondent on the expert panel in the Sunday Times Enterprise Network feature.

About the Contributors

Robert Sutton is the Professor of Management Science and Engineering at Stanford University. At Stanford he co-leads the Center for Work, Technology, and Organization and is a faculty member in the Stanford Technology Ventures Program.

A former Professor of Haas Business School, he has been at Stanford since joining in 1983 after completing his PhD at the University of Michigan.

Over the last twenty years, he has been developing the simple core message that long-term performance is dependent upon on having a number of good ideas that are subsequently implemented.

A prolific writer, Professor Sutton has authored *Weird Ideas That Work*, and is coauthor of *The Knowing-Doing Gap* and *Hard Facts, Dangerous Half-Truths, and Total Nonsense: Profiting from Evidence-Based Management* (with Jeffrey Pfeffer).

Professor Sutton teaches in Stanford's professional education program. He also consults with a number of global blue-chip companies, including Ernst & Young, The Cap, Hewlett-Packard Development Co., IBMCorp., McDonald's Corp., Pepsi-Co Inc., Procter & Gamble Co., and Xerox Corp.

He has been a Fellow of the Center for Advanced Study in the Behavioral Sciences in 1986–1987, 1994–1995, and 2002–2003.

Sir David Varney has held a variety of senior roles within the oil organization Shell, including the position of Managing Director of AB Svenska Shell in Sweden and Director of Shell International with responsibility for Shell's Oil Products business in Europe.

He was Chief Executive Officer of BG Group (formerly British Gas) from 1996 to 2000, where his experience spanned both the U.K. and overseas markets.

In 2001 he became Chairman of mm02, the provider of mobile communications services.

From September 2004 to August 2006, he was Executive Chairman of HM Revenue and Customs, the new department created from the integration of HM Customs and Excise and the Inland Revenue. Sir David chaired Business in the Community from 2002 to 2004 and was President of the Chartered Institute of Management for 2005/2006.

Sir David is also President of the Council for the Institute of Employment Studies. He currently serves as the Prime Minister's Advisor on Public Service Transformation

Jimmy Wales is the Founder of Wikipedia, the free open-content encyclopedia.

From 1994 to 2000 Mr. Wales was the Research Director at Chicago Options Associates, a futures and options trading firm in Chicago. In 2000 he started the open-content encyclopedia Nupedia. In 2001 he founded Wikipedia, a free, online encyclopedia that anyone can edit.

Mr. Wales is the Chairman of Wikimedia Foundation, Inc., a nonprofit charitable organization dedicated to encouraging the growth, development, and distribution of free, multilingual content. He is the Co-Founder of Wiki, Inc., a wiki farm that includes collection of wikis on different topics, all hosted on the same site.

He is a Fellow at the Berkman Center for Internet & Society at Harvard Law School and a Director of Socialtext, a leading provider of Enterprise 2.0 solutions. He is also Director of Creative Commons, a nonprofit licensing organization.

In 2006 Mr. Wales was named as one of *Time* magazine's people who shape our world, and in 2007 he was named as a *Forbes* magazine Web celebrity.

Will Whitehorn is the President of Virgin Galactic.

Mr. Whitehorn's early career included time as a helicopter crewman in the North Sea for British Airways. He was also a Market Intelligence Officer for the TSB Group flotation and a graduate trainee with Thomas Cook Group.

Additionally, he was an Account Director at Lombard Communications, where he worked on numerous flotations and bids for companies including Chrysalis Group, Ward White, and Grampian Holdings.

Mr. Whitehorn joined Virgin Group in 1987 as Head of Corporate Public Relations. In 2002 he became Virgin Group's Brand Development and Corporate Affairs Director, in this role acting as Sir Richard Branson's spokesman. He was also respon-

sible for the corporate image of Virgin, public affairs, global brand development, selected company
stewardship, and a number of new business development activities. In 2004 he was appointed President of Virgin Galactic.

In 2004 he became a Non-Executive Chairman
for Next Fifteen Communications Plc., a worldwide
technology public relations group.

⊰ ACKNOWLEDGMENTS ⊱

First and foremost, a heartfelt thanks goes to all of the executives who have candidly shared their hard-earned experience and battle-tested insights for the Lessons Learned series.

Angelia Herrin at Harvard Business School Publishing consistently offered unwavering support, good humor, and counsel from the inception of this ambitious project.

Brian Surette, Hollis Heimbouch, and David Goehring provided invaluable editorial direction, perspective, and encouragement. Much appreciation goes to Jennifer Lynn for her research and diligent attention to detail. Many thanks to the entire HBSP team of designers, copy editors, and marketing professionals who helped bring this series to life.

Finally, thanks to our fellow cofounder James MacKinnon and the entire Fifty

Acknowledgments

Lessons team for the tremendous amount of time, effort, and steadfast support for this project.

—Adam Sodowick
Andy Hasoon
Directors and Cofounders
Fifty Lessons